FORTNITE

KENNY ABDO

Fly!
An Imprint of Abdo Zoom
abdobooks.com

abdobooks.com

Published by Abdo Zoom, a division of ABDO, P.O. Box 398166, Minneapolis, Minnesota 55439. Copyright © 2023 by Abdo Consulting Group, Inc. International copyrights reserved in all countries. No part of this book may be reproduced in any form without written permission from the publisher. Fly!™ is a trademark and logo of Abdo Zoom.

Printed in the United States of America, North Mankato, Minnesota.
052022
092022

THIS BOOK CONTAINS RECYCLED MATERIALS

Photo Credits: Alamy, AP Images, Getty Images, Shutterstock, ©BagoGames p.cover / CC BY 2.0, ©Sergey Galyonkin p.9/ CC BY-SA 2.0
Production Contributors: Kenny Abdo, Jennie Forsberg, Grace Hansen
Design Contributors: Candice Keimig, Neil Klinepier

Library of Congress Control Number: 2021950298

Publisher's Cataloging-in-Publication Data

Names: Abdo, Kenny, author.
Title: Fortnite / by Kenny Abdo.
Description: Minneapolis, Minnesota : Abdo Zoom, 2023 | Series: Esports |
    Includes online resources and index.
Identifiers: ISBN 9781098228477 (lib. bdg.) | ISBN 9781644947838 (pbk.) |
    ISBN 9781098229313 (ebook) | ISBN 9781098229733 (Read-to-Me ebook)
Subjects: LCSH: Video games--Juvenile literature. | eSports (Contests)--Juvenile
    literature. | Fortnite Battle Royale (Game)--Juvenile literature. | Epic Games,
    Inc.--Juvenile literature. | Imaginary wars and battles--Juvenile literature.
Classification: DDC 794.8--dc23

TABLE OF CONTENTS

FORTNITE

Fortnite has captured the imaginations of more than 350 million players around the globe!

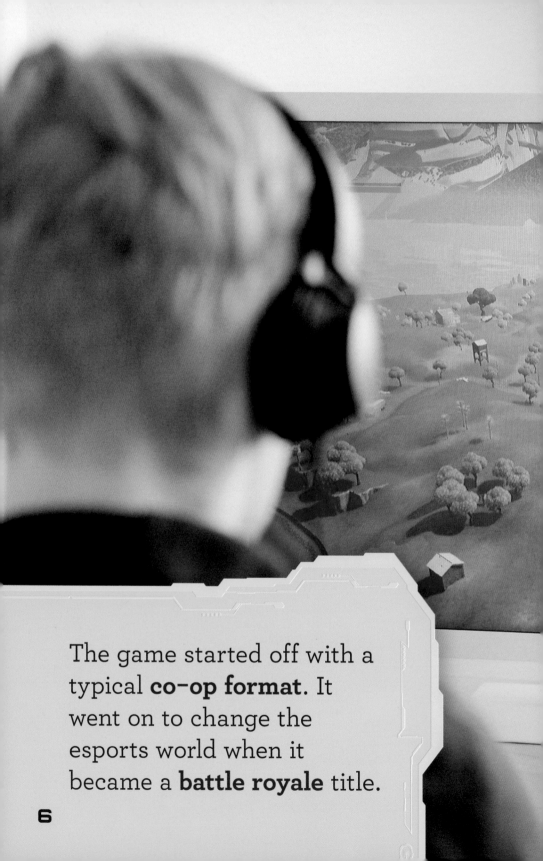

The game started off with a typical **co-op format.** It went on to change the esports world when it became a **battle royale** title.

Video game developer Epic Games began toying with the idea of *Fortnite* in 2011. It wanted to take elements from popular games like *Minecraft* and add a role-playing mode.

PlayerUnknown's Battlegrounds (PUBG) became a worldwide hit in 2017. Epic wanted to take what it had with *Fortnite* and add **battle royale** gameplay like *PUBG*.

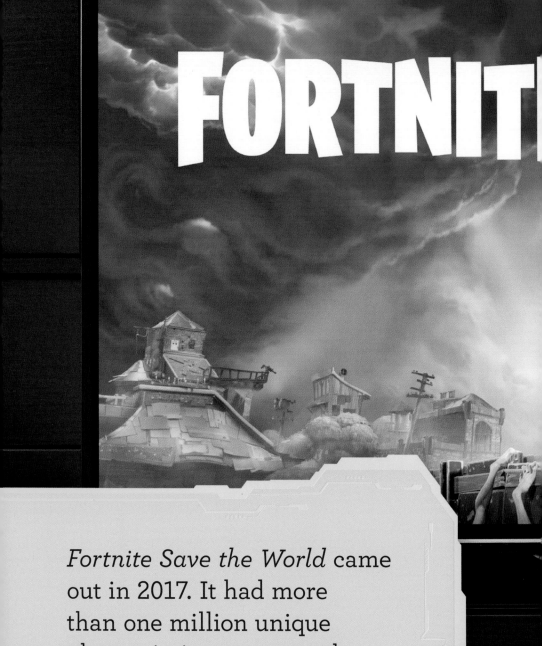

Fortnite Save the World came out in 2017. It had more than one million unique players in just one month. *Fortnite Battle Royale* quickly followed and had 10 million players within two weeks.

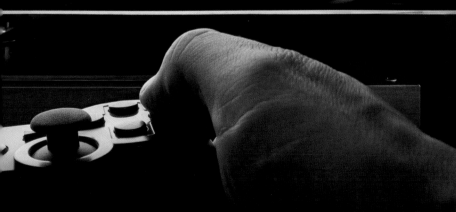

JOURNEY

In 2018, famous **streamer** Ninja broke viewer count records. Playing with Travis Scott, Drake, and other celebrities, the superstar stream skyrocketed *Fortnite's* fame.

The first Fortnite Pro-Am competition was held at the 2018 E3 conference. It was won by Ninja and DJ Marshmello. They donated $1 million of the prize money to **charity.**

Later that year, Epic Games began hosting a **Summer Skirmish** series. Each week had a different **format**. A second competition series, the **Fall Skirmish**, shortly followed.

The 2019 Fortnite World Cup was one of the biggest events in esports history. Kyle Giersdorf walked away with $3 million. Just 16 years old at the time, he beat 99 other players!

In 2020, Epic began sponsoring high school and college-level *Fortnite* **tournaments**. Teaming up with PlayVS, all students can play and compete for free.

The Fortnite World Cup is big. The $3 million top prize beats the winnings in many major events, like Wimbledon, the Indianapolis 500, and the Masters!

Fortnite has proven to be one of the most successful **battle royale** games in history. And it will continue to **dominate** the esports arena.

GLOSSARY

battle royale – a competition between many participants that goes until there is only one left.

charity – an organization set up to provide help and raise money for those in need.

co-op – short for cooperative, a type of video game that allows players to work together as a team.

dominate – to be much more powerful or successful than others.

Fall Skirmish – a 6-week series of *Fortnite* competitions between September and October.

format – the way a game is set up with rules and guidelines.

streamer – a person who broadcasts themselves in real time while playing video games.

Summer Skirmish – an 8-week series of *Fortnite* competitions between July and September.

tournament – a set of games or matches held to find a first-place winner.

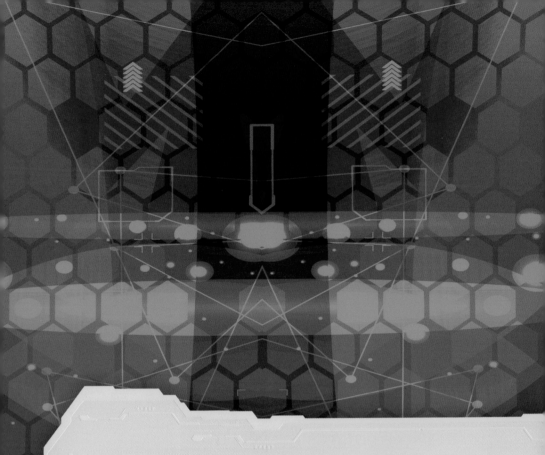

ONLINE RESOURCES

Booklinks
NONFICTION NETWORK
FREE! ONLINE NONFICTION RESOURCES

To learn more about Fortnite, please visit **abdobooklinks.com** or scan this QR code. These links are routinely monitored and updated to provide the most current information available.

INDEX